The Gospel of Thomas

The Timeless Teachings of Hidden Wisdom and Spiritual Truth

A Modern Translation

Adapted for the Contemporary Reader

Thomas the Apostle

Translated by Tim Zengerink

© **Copyright 2025**
All rights reserved.

It is not legal to reproduce, duplicate, or transmit any part of this document in either electronic means or in printed format. Recording of this publication is strictly prohibited and any storage of this document is not allowed unless with written permission from the publisher except for the use of brief quotations in a book review.

This book contains works of fiction. Any resemblance to persons living or dead, or places, events, or locations is purely coincidental.

Table Of Contents

Preface - Message to the Reader 1

Introduction 5

The Gospel of Thomas 13

Thank You for Reading 25

Preface - Message to the Reader

What If You Could Help Rebuild the Greatest Library in Human History?

Thousands of years ago, the Library of Alexandria stood as the crown jewel of human achievement — a sanctuary where the collected wisdom of every known civilization was gathered, preserved, and shared freely.

And then, it was lost.

Through fire, conquest, and the slow erosion of time, humanity lost not just books — but ideas, dreams, discoveries, and stories that could have changed the world forever.

Today, the Library of Alexandria lives again — and you are invited to be a part of its restoration.

Our mission is simple yet profound:

To rebuild the greatest library the world has ever known, and to translate all timeless works into every language and dialect, so that no seeker of knowledge is ever left behind again.

By joining our movement to rebuild the modern Library of Alexandria, you become part of an unprecedented mission:

- **Unlimited Access to the Greatest Audiobooks & eBooks Ever Written**

  Instantly explore thousands of legendary works—Plato, Shakespeare, Jane Austen, Leo Tolstoy, and countless more. All instantly available to read or listen, placing a complete literary universe at your fingertips.

- **Beautiful Paperback & Deluxe Editions at Printing Cost**

  Own any title as an elegant paperback, deluxe hardcover, or stunning collectible boxset—offered to you at true printing cost, delivered straight to your door. Build your personal Library of Alexandria, crafted for beauty, built for durability, and worthy of proud display.

- **Fresh Translations for Modern Readers—in Every Language & Dialect**

  Enjoy timeless masterpieces reimagined in clear, contemporary language—no more outdated phrases or obscure references. Alongside the original versions, we're tirelessly translating these classics into every language and dialect imaginable, ensuring accessibility and understanding across cultures and generations.

- **Join a Global Renaissance of Literature & Knowledge**

    You directly support expanding our library, publishing deluxe editions at true cost, translating works into all global languages, and bringing humanity's greatest stories to people everywhere. By joining today, you're not just preserving a legacy of masterpieces; you set in motion a powerful wave of literary accessibility.

Become a Torchbearer of Knowledge.

Join us for free now at **LibraryofAlexandria.com**

Together, we will ensure that the light of human wisdom never fades again.

With gratitude and a shared love of knowledge,

The Modern Library of Alexandria Team

Visit:

www.libraryofalexandria.com

Or scan the code below:

Introduction

Across the vast landscape of early Christianity, amidst the diverse texts and teachings of the faith, one extraordinary manuscript stands distinctly apart—the enigmatic and profound Gospel of Thomas. Unlike the canonical Gospels of Matthew, Mark, Luke, and John, which present narratives of Jesus' life, miracles, and crucifixion, The Gospel of Thomas offers a unique collection of 114 sayings attributed directly to Jesus, unembellished by story or historical context. These teachings invite readers into a deeper, more personal exploration of spiritual insight, divine wisdom, and inner enlightenment.

Attributed traditionally to Thomas the Apostle—famously known as "Doubting Thomas" from canonical scripture—this gospel resonates with a profound authenticity and intimate immediacy. Its teachings challenge conventional understandings, inviting readers to uncover spiritual truths through contemplation, introspection, and the realization that the divine kingdom resides within each individual.

Translated by Tim Zengerink

Historical Discovery and Significance

The Gospel of Thomas remained lost to the world for centuries, hidden beneath desert sands until its remarkable discovery in 1945 among the Nag Hammadi manuscripts in Egypt. This ancient trove of texts profoundly altered scholarly understanding of early Christianity by revealing a diverse spiritual landscape that existed alongside, and often in tension with, the established orthodox traditions. Among these findings, The Gospel of Thomas emerged prominently, sparking renewed scholarly and spiritual interest due to its unique teachings and its profound philosophical implications.

Though scholars date The Gospel of Thomas between the first and second centuries CE, its origins and exact historical context remain subjects of vibrant academic debate. Some suggest it might even preserve sayings of Jesus older than those in the canonical Gospels, possibly reflecting an earlier and more original tradition. Regardless of its precise origin, the spiritual power, depth, and directness of its teachings have resonated deeply with readers and seekers around the world.

The Unique Format of Sayings

The Gospel of Thomas does not follow a narrative or chronological structure. Instead, it presents Jesus' teachings in succinct, profound statements known as logia. These aphorisms vary from clear and direct ethical instructions to enigmatic and mystical statements designed to provoke deep reflection and self-exploration.

This format invites readers into an active, contemplative dialogue. Each saying serves as a spiritual puzzle or koan, meant not merely to be understood intellectually but experienced internally and spiritually. The very structure encourages meditation and introspection, fostering personal revelation and spiritual awakening.

Core Themes and Spiritual Insights

Several profound themes emerge consistently throughout The Gospel of Thomas, illuminating timeless spiritual truths and inviting readers toward a transformative journey of self-discovery and enlightenment:

1. The Kingdom Within

Perhaps the most revolutionary teaching of The Gospel of Thomas is its emphasis on discovering the divine kingdom within oneself. Jesus teaches that the kingdom of God is not a distant reality to await passively, but a present, internal experience accessible through self-awareness, spiritual insight, and inner transformation. This powerful message challenges traditional religious views, emphasizing direct, personal spiritual experience over external ritual or dogma.

2. Self-Knowledge and Enlightenment

Repeatedly, The Gospel of Thomas emphasizes the profound connection between self-knowledge and spiritual enlightenment. Jesus instructs that true spiritual awakening begins with deeply understanding oneself, asserting that genuine insight into the divine emerges through inner reflection and personal realization.

3. The Unity of All Existence

Another central teaching within The Gospel of Thomas is the interconnectedness and unity of all existence. Jesus speaks of transcending dualistic perceptions of reality, encouraging readers to recognize the divine essence that permeates all creation. This wisdom aligns closely with mystical traditions across various spiritual paths, resonating deeply with those seeking universal truths.

4. Radical Simplicity and Authentic Living

Many sayings emphasize living authentically, free from external pressures, material attachments, and superficial concerns. Jesus encourages simplicity, humility, and authenticity as pathways toward spiritual freedom and true fulfillment. These teachings hold significant relevance today, offering powerful guidance amidst the complexities of contemporary life.

The Gospel's Relevance for Modern Readers

In today's rapidly evolving spiritual landscape, The Gospel of Thomas holds exceptional relevance. Contemporary seekers, often disillusioned by dogmatic traditions yet deeply committed to personal growth and spirituality, find profound resonance with its teachings. The gospel's emphasis on direct, personal spiritual experience, inner transformation, and universal truths transcends religious boundaries, appealing broadly to individuals from diverse backgrounds and spiritual paths.

The timeless nature of these teachings provides practical guidance on navigating modern life's complexities and stresses. Themes of inner peace, authenticity, and spiritual awakening speak directly to the challenges and opportunities faced by contemporary readers, offering transformative insights that foster personal empowerment and spiritual liberation.

Importance of This Modern Translation

This modern translation and adaptation of The Gospel of Thomas carefully balances preserving the original text's depth, poetic beauty, and mystical power with the accessibility and clarity needed by contemporary readers. Complex, enigmatic sayings have been thoughtfully rendered into language that remains true to their spiritual essence while removing unnecessary linguistic barriers.

By making this profound wisdom more accessible, readers from diverse spiritual backgrounds can deeply engage with and apply the gospel's transformative teachings to their lives. Whether approached as historical scripture, spiritual wisdom, or philosophical meditation, this translation ensures each reader can embark confidently and clearly upon their journey of self-discovery and spiritual awakening.

Embarking on Your Personal Spiritual Journey

As you begin your exploration of The Gospel of Thomas, you enter into a profound spiritual dialogue transcending historical and religious boundaries. Each saying within this gospel invites deep reflection, offering keys to unlock inner truths and divine wisdom already present within you.

Approach this text not merely as an intellectual or historical curiosity, but as a living spiritual guide. Allow yourself space and time to meditate upon each saying, reflecting deeply upon its personal meaning and significance. Trust your inner responses, insights, and realizations, knowing these teachings aim to awaken the divine spark already residing within you.

Embrace the Journey

The Gospel of Thomas invites you to embark on a transformative spiritual journey toward self-discovery, enlightenment, and divine connection. Its timeless teachings challenge, inspire, and guide, empowering you to realize profound spiritual truths and live authentically aligned with your highest potential.

May your engagement with The Gospel of Thomas illuminate your path, awaken your inner wisdom, and

Translated by Tim Zengerink

inspire a deeper connection to the divine essence that permeates all life. Embrace this timeless wisdom, and let its powerful teachings transform your understanding of yourself, your world, and your spiritual purpose.

The Gospel of Thomas

The hidden words spoken by the Savior to Judas Thomas, which I, Mathaias, wrote down as I walked with them, listening to their conversation.

The Savior said, "Brother Thomas, while you are still in this world, listen carefully to my words. I will reveal the answers to the thoughts you have kept inside. Since people say you are my twin and my true companion, take a moment to look within yourself. Learn who you really are, understand your existence, and discover how you have come to be. Since you are called my brother, you should not remain unaware of your true nature.

"I see that you have already begun to understand because you recognize that I bring the knowledge of truth. Even though you walk with me and do not yet fully comprehend everything, you have already started to know. Because of this, you will be called 'the one who knows himself.' For the person who does not know themselves knows nothing, but the one who comes to understand themselves also gains insight into the deep mysteries of all things. Therefore, my brother Thomas, you have seen what is hidden from most people—things that they stumble over in their ignorance."

Thomas replied, "Lord, I ask you to answer the questions I carry in my heart before you leave this world. When I hear you speak of hidden truths, I will be able to share them. But I realize now that understanding and living the truth is not easy for people."

The Savior answered, "If even the things you can see are unclear and confusing to you, how will you understand when I speak of things that are unseen? If the works of truth that are obvious in this world are already difficult for you to follow, how can you hope to carry out the actions that belong to the higher realms and the fullness of divine perfection, which are beyond human sight? How, then, will you be known as true 'workers' of the truth? For now, you are still like students who have not yet reached completion."

Thomas said to him, "Master, please tell us more about these things that are hidden from our understanding."

The Savior replied, "All living bodies, including animals, come into existence through natural birth. Their origins are clear, as is their nature. In the same way, the things that belong to the higher realms, though not visible in the same way, exist through their own roots. These roots produce fruit that sustains them. The bodies you see in this world, however, survive by consuming other living beings, creating a cycle of change. But this change leads to decay and death because these bodies do not hold the hope of eternal life. They are like the animals—they perish in the same way. If their origin is the same, how can they create anything different? This is why you are still like children until you reach a greater understanding."

Thomas then said, "This is why I say, Lord, that those who try to explain hidden and difficult matters are like people shooting arrows at a target in the dark. They aim and shoot as if they can see the target, but they do not truly know where it is. But when the light appears and removes the darkness, their efforts will become clear. And you, our light, reveal the truth to us, O Lord."

The Savior said, "Light finds its existence within light."

Thomas asked, "Lord, why does the light we see, which shines for people, rise and set every day?"

The Savior answered, "Thomas, this light exists for your sake—not so you can stay in this world forever, but so you can find your way out of it. When all who are chosen have turned away from their earthly desires, this light will return to its source, and its true essence will welcome it back because it has faithfully done its work."

The Savior continued, "Oh, the deep love of the true light! But also, how fierce is the fire that burns inside human bodies and bones! This fire is in them day and night, consuming their strength, clouding their thoughts, and leading their souls into confusion. It stirs up desires, both seen and unseen, pushing men toward women and women toward men.

"This is why it is said, 'Whoever seeks the truth from true wisdom must create wings for themselves so they can fly and escape the desires that control people.' He must rise above every earthly craving and free himself from the pull of the physical world."

Thomas said, "Lord, this is exactly what I want to understand, for I see that you are the one who brings true knowledge and guidance."

The Savior replied, "We must talk about these things because they are meant for those who are working toward perfection. If you want to be perfect, you must think about these truths and follow them. If you do not, then you will be called 'foolish,' for a wise person cannot live in harmony with someone who refuses to understand. A wise person grows in knowledge, while a fool sees no difference between good and bad. To the fool, they are the same. But the wise man is nourished by truth, and as the scripture says, 'He will be like a tree planted beside flowing water,' always growing and strengthened by the waters of life.

"But some, even though they have the ability to rise above, still chase after things they can see, things far from the truth. They are deceived by the fire that guides them—it looks like light, but it is only an illusion. This fire shines with a temporary beauty, attracting them with its charm. It tricks them with pleasure, trapping them in a false sense of happiness. It blinds them with endless desires, burning their souls with cravings they cannot escape. It is like a sharp stake driven into their hearts, something they cannot pull out.

"This fire, like a bridle in their mouths, controls them and steers their actions according to its will. It binds them with chains, wrapping itself around every part of them. It traps them in the suffering of wanting things that will fade away, things that constantly change and never satisfy. These people are pulled downward by their desires, consumed by them. In the end, they become like animals in this temporary world, no different from everything else that is destined to decay."

Thomas thought about this and said, "It is true, just as it is said, 'Many do not understand the truth of their own soul.'"

The Savior answered, "Blessed is the wise person who searches for truth. When he finds it, he will rest in it forever. No one will be able to shake him or make him afraid, for he will be standing on a foundation that cannot be moved."

Thomas then asked, "Lord, is it good for us to stay among people who are like us?"

The Savior said, "Yes, it is good to find peace among those who share the truth. The things people see and hold onto in this world will not last forever. Their bodies will break down and return to the earth, just like everything else that is physical. When that happens, the fire they once feared will become their suffering, fueled by their attachment to their old way of life. They will be trapped by what is visible, unable to rise beyond it.

"And those who look toward the unseen but do not truly love the truth will also perish. Their focus on worldly things will consume them, and the fire within them will destroy their souls. Soon, all that can be seen will fade away, and from its remains, only empty shadows will rise—lost souls. These souls will remain in suffering, clinging to lifeless bodies, tormented by corruption and despair."

Thomas asked, "What should we say to these people? How can we speak to those who cannot see the truth? What message should we share with those who say, 'We came to do good, not to bring curses,' yet also claim, 'If we had not been born into the flesh, we would not have known sin'?"

The Savior answered, "You must not think of such people as truly human. They are like wild animals, consuming each other with their actions. They are blind to the kingdom of light because they are drawn to the deceptive sweetness of the fire. They serve death, rushing toward corruption, following the desires of those who came before them—those who sought destruction. These people will fall into the abyss, where they will suffer the consequences of their wickedness. They will be overcome with confusion and despair, wanting to escape their own bodies but unable to do so peacefully.

"They take pleasure in their own madness without realizing it. They blindly follow their own distorted thinking, convinced they are wise. Their entire being—body, mind, and soul—is consumed by their selfish desires. They focus only on their own actions, but in the end, the fire will devour them. It will burn away their illusions, leaving them in great suffering."

Thomas asked, "Lord, what will happen to those who are cast down among them? My heart is heavy because many struggle against them."

The Savior looked at him and said, "What do you think, Thomas? What is your own understanding?"

Judas, called Thomas, answered, "Lord, it is for you to speak, and for me to listen and learn."

The Savior replied, "Then listen carefully and believe in the truth of what I say. Both the one who plants the seed and the seed itself will pass away, for everything must go through the fire. Both fire and water will consume them, and they will find themselves trapped in darkness. Over time, they will bear the bitter fruit of wickedness. Their judgment will come, and they will be destroyed by the very things they once fed—the beasts, the people, and even the forces of nature: the rain, the wind, the air, and the light above."

Thomas said, "Lord, your words have convinced us. We know in our hearts that they are true. But the world will not understand them. To them, your words will sound foolish, even laughable. How, then, can we go out and teach these things? The world does not respect us."

The Savior said, "I tell you the truth, those who hear your words but turn away in mockery, who laugh at the truth you share, will not escape judgment. Such people will be handed over to the ruler above, the one who has power over all others. This ruler will cast them down from heaven into the abyss, where they will be trapped in darkness, unable to move or escape. The depths of suffering will surround them, and there will be no forgiveness, no relief from their torment.

"The angel of punishment, Tartarouchos, will chase them, striking them with whips of fire that send sparks into their faces. No matter where they run, the fire will follow them. If they try to flee west, the flames will block their way. If they turn south, the fire will rise before them. If they go north, the burning heat will still be there. Even if they turn east, they will find no escape, for they did not seek refuge while they were alive. How will they find it when the day of judgment arrives?"

The Savior continued, "How terrible it will be for those who live without hope, who trust in things that will never come true.

"How terrible for those who put their faith in the flesh and cling to this dying world! How long will you remain blind? How long will you foolishly believe that what is eternal will also pass away? You have tied your hope to this world, and you treat this short life as your god! By doing so, you have ruined your own souls.

"How terrible for those consumed by the fire of desire, for it will never be satisfied.

"How terrible for those trapped in an endless cycle of struggle, unable to break free.

"How terrible for those who are burned by desires that destroy their bodies and poison their souls. These flames prepare them for a dreadful fate alongside others who will suffer the same."

Translated by Tim Zengerink

How terrible for those who are prisoners in the darkness they have chosen! You laugh, but your laughter is empty. Your joy is wild and meaningless. You do not even realize your own downfall. You do not stop to think about your condition. You do not see that you live in darkness and walk in the shadow of death. Instead, you are consumed by the fire within you, fooled by its illusion of warmth and comfort. You have been blinded by your own desires, taking pleasure in the very things that destroy you. You find sweetness in the poison that is killing you, and you welcome the suffering caused by your own choices. You have traded freedom for chains, filling your hearts with emptiness and your minds with foolish thoughts. The fire of your own making has surrounded you with smoke, hiding the light from your eyes. You have wrapped yourselves in falsehood, trusting in things that will never last.

Do you not see that you live among those who seek to harm you? They do not see you as equals but as something to use. You have washed your souls in the water of darkness, following your desires without realizing the traps all around you. How terrible for you who have chosen lies over truth! You fail to understand that the sun, which sees everything, is watching and will one day bring justice. Even the moon sees what happens in the night and day, witnessing the actions of all people.

How terrible for those who chase after fleeting pleasures, letting their desires rule over them. How terrible for those who let their own bodies control them, for these desires will only bring suffering. How terrible for those who give in to evil spirits, letting their passions burn uncontrollably. Who will bring cool water to quench their inner fire? Who will shine a light to break the darkness inside them? Who will cleanse the polluted waters of their soul?

The sun, the moon, the air, the spirit, the earth, and the water all give life to the world. But if the sun does not shine on these things, they will dry up and die like weeds. The weeds grow wild and unchecked, choking out everything good around them. But when the grapevine is planted, it grows strong and spreads its shade over the land. It overtakes the weeds and brush, turning the soil into something rich and full of life. The vine grows healthy and full, bringing joy to its master, who no longer has to struggle against the weeds. The vine restores the land, making it fertile and abundant.

Jesus continued, saying, "How terrible for those who have rejected the truth! You work hard, but without understanding, and you rush toward your own destruction. You try to silence those who speak about life and truth, but even when you kill them, they rise again to testify against your ways.

"Blessed are those who see the dangers ahead and turn away from them.

"Blessed are those who suffer rejection and mockery because they love the Lord.

"Blessed are those who weep under the weight of suffering, for they will be set free and find peace.

"Stay alert and pray, so you do not remain trapped in the flesh. Break free from the chains of bitterness that tie you to this world. In prayer, you will find rest, leaving behind the pain and shame of this life. When you are freed from the struggles and desires of the body, you will enter the eternal rest that the Good One has prepared for you. You will reign with the King, united with him as he is with you, now and forever."

The Book of Thomas the Contender ends with this:

Remember me, my brothers and sisters, in your prayers. Peace be with the saints and with all who walk in the Spirit.

Thank You for Reading

Dear Reader,

We hope this timeless classic has sparked your imagination and enriched your literary journey. Now that you've turned the final page, we want to share a vision for the future of reading—one where every classic you've ever wanted to explore is at your fingertips, in a format that best suits your life.

We'd like to invite you to gain immediate, unlimited digital & audiobook access to hundreds of the most treasured literary classics ever written—along with the option to secure deluxe paperback, hardcover & box set editions at printing cost. Together, we can spark a new global literary renaissance alongside our small, independent publishing house called "The Library of Alexandria."

Thousands of years ago, the Library of Alexandria stood as a beacon of knowledge—until it was lost to history. We aim to reignite that spirit of preservation and discovery right now, in the modern age—only this time, it's accessible to all, in every language and every format.

Picture a world where every timeless classic, novel, poem, or philosophical treatise is not only available to read but also updated for today's readers—modernized, translated into any language or dialect, and ready to enjoy in any format you choose, whether that is in an eBook, audiobook, paperback, or deluxe hardcover & box set version a printing cost.

By joining our movement to rebuild the modern Library of Alexandria, you become part of an unprecedented mission to offer:

- **Unlimited Audiobook & eBook Access to the Greatest Classics of All Time**

    Instantly explore thousands of legendary works, from Plato and Shakespeare to Jane Austen and Leo Tolstoy. All are instantly ready to read or listen to, giving you a complete literary universe at your fingertips.

- **Paperback & Deluxe Editions at Printing Costs:**

    Purchase any title in a paperback, deluxe hardbound, or deluxe boxset edition at printing costs, shipped right to your doorstep. Curate your personal library of Alexandria with editions worthy of display—crafted to last, designed to captivate, and delivered straight to your door.

- **Modern translations for Contemporary Readers in all languages and dialects**

  Discover a vast selection of classics reimagined in clear, current language—no more struggling with outdated phrases or obscure references. Next to the original versions, we aim to offer translations in as many languages and dialects as possible.

  As we continue our translation efforts and add new languages, readers everywhere can connect with these works as if they were written today. By bridging linguistic divides, you're contributing to ensuring that these timeless stories become more meaningful, accessible, and inspiring for people across the globe.

- **Your Personal Library of Alexandria:**

  Over the months and years, you'll curate a unique physical archive of classics—each volume a testament to your taste, curiosity, and love of knowledge. It's not just about owning books—it's about curating a cultural legacy you'll cherish and pass down for generations to come.

- **Join a Global Literary Renaissance:**

  Your support fuels an ongoing mission: allowing us to reinvest in offering deluxe print editions (including special boxsets) at their true cost, broaden the range of available formats and translations, and extend the reach of these works to new audiences worldwide. By joining today, you're not just preserving a legacy of masterpieces; you set in motion a powerful wave of literary accessibility.

We are more than a publisher—we're a movement, and we can't do it alone. Your support lets us scale our mission, preserving and reimagining history's greatest works for tomorrow's readers.

Become a Torchbearer of knowledge.

Thank you for picking up this book and allowing us into your literary journey. As you turn the pages, know that you're part of something larger: a global effort to keep these stories alive, share their wisdom across borders and generations, and spark a true cultural revival for the modern era.

If this resonates with you—please consider taking the next step by visiting:

www.libraryofalexandria.com

With gratitude and a shared love of knowledge,

The Modern Library of Alexandria Team

Visit:

www.libraryofalexandria.com

Or scan the code below:

www.ingramcontent.com/pod-product-compliance
Lightning Source LLC
LaVergne TN
LVHW030631080426
835512LV00021B/3464